MW01118978

CALIFORNIA WINE COUNTRY RESTAURANTS

Local Editor: Meesha Halm

Local Coordinator: Maura Sell

Editor: Troy Segal

Published and distributed by
ZAGAT SURVEY, LLC
4 Columbus Circle
New York, New York 10019
Tel: 212 977 6000
E-mail: californiawine@zagat.com
Web site: www.zagat.com

Acknowledgments

We'd like to thank Antonia Allegra, Laurie Armstrong, Mark Carter, Sarah Cummings, Heidi Cusick, Jon and Olive Poe Fox, D.K. Jackson, Michelle Anna Jordan, Vincent and Conor Logan, Mary Orlin, Laura Reiley and Willow Waldeck.

This guide would not have been possible without the hard work of our staff, especially Reni Chin, Anna Chlumsky, Jeff Freier, Jessica Gonzalez, Katherine Harris, Diane Karlin, Natalie Lebert, Mike Liao, Dave Makulec, Laura Mitchell, Rob Poole, Robert Seixas, Yoji Yamaguchi and Sharon Yates.

What's New

Everyone knows that the valleys of Napa, Sonoma and Mendocino are home to some of the nation's finest vintners. But they also offer some of the Golden State's choicest restaurants, now thriving thanks to a post-9/11 surge in regional travel. To acknowledge this epicurean excellence, Zagat has spun off its first-ever *California Wine Country* guide, which includes both excerpts from our *2003 San Francisco Restaurant Survey* and a select list of wineries.

Napa Nibbles: Long considered the sleepy stepchild of the Valley, Downtown Napa awoke this year. The debut of the COPIA Center and its flagship Julia's Kitchen, a Cal–New French named for museum trustee Julia Child, started the momentum, which quickened with the arrival of tapas-touting Zuzu. The scene should only get hotter in the late summer with the scheduled opening of the Vintner's Collective Tasting Room, an 1875 building-turned-showcase for local artisinal producers, and the renovated Napa Mill complex. The Mill will house the relocated Celadon and Angele, a new country French from Auberge du Soleil's proprietor. Farther up valley, Martini House has become a happening spot in St. Helena, offering New American cuisine in a hunting-lodge setting.

Savoring Sonoma: The big news is that chef Charlie Palmer (of NYC's and Las Vegas' Aureole) has relocated to Healdsburg with his Dry Creek Kitchen, which showcases local ingredients and wines. Over at the Sonoma Mission Inn, the made-over Santé's new spa menu now enables big eaters to actually enjoy dropping pounds.

Mendocino Meals: Just as wine lovers are discovering Mendocino County, foodies have begun to recognize North Coast dining. Three years ago, the *SF Survey* reviewed three Mendocino restaurants. This year, we include 20, from Sharon's by the Sea, a humble seafooder, to the grandly historic Victorian Gardens, which prepares Italian feasts for a lucky few each evening.

August 6, 2002   Meesha Halm

Top 50 Food Rankings

Excluding restaurants with low voting

29 French Laundry/N*
27 Terra/N
   La Toque/N
26 Bistro Jeanty/N
   Hana Japanese/S
   Cafe La Haye/S
   Domaine Chandon/N
   Restaurant/Stevenswood/M
   Tastings Restaurant/S
   Auberge du Soleil/N
25 Syrah/S
   Madrona Manor/S
   Cafe Beaujolais/M
   Julia's Kitchen/N
   Tra Vigne/N
   Albion River Inn/M
   Downtown Bakery/S
   Cafe Lolo/S
24 Rendezvous Inn/M
   Dry Creek Kitchen/S
   Taylor's Automatic/N
   Bistro Don Giovanni/N
   Foothill Cafe/N
   Kenwood/S
   Ravenous/Ravenette/S

   John Ash & Co./S
   Martini House/N
   Applewood Inn/S
   St. Orres/M
23 MacCallum House/M
   Mustards Grill/N
   All Season's Cafe/N
   Bouchon/N
   Restaurant at Meadowood/N
   Gary Chu/S
   Manzanita/S
   Celadon/N
   Santi/S
22 Chateau Souverain Café/S
   Ledford House/M
   Lisa Hemenway's Bistro/S
   Rutherford Grill/N
   Feast/S
   Zuzu/N
   Pinot Blanc/N
   Wine Spectator Greystone/N
   Moosse Cafe/M
   Mixx Restaurant/S
   955 Ukiah/M
21 Cole's Chop House/N

---

* N=Napa County; S=Sonoma County; M=Mendocino County

Top Food Rankings

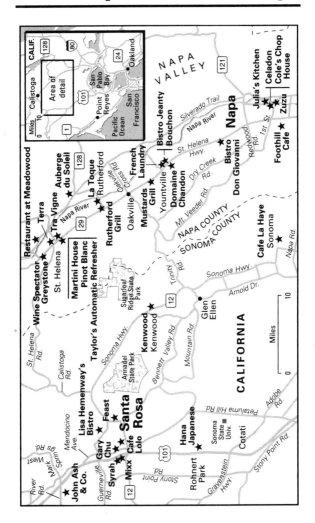

Top Food Rankings

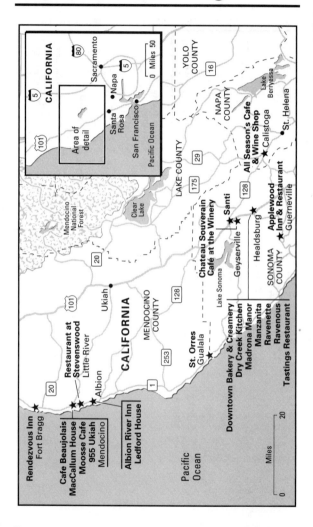

Key to Ratings/Symbols

Name, Address & Phone Number   **Zagat Ratings**

Hours & Credit Cards

	F	D	S	C
Tim & Nina's ◑ⓈⒹ⊄	▽ 23	9	13	$15

9999 Lincoln Ave. (Washington St.), Calistoga, 707-555-1234

◪ Open "more or less when T & N feel like it", this Calistoga cafe literally offers a "down-and-dirty dining" experience (it's "housed in a hut" made of the local mud); comprised exclusively of local produce, the Californian food "tastes fresh off the vine"; trouble is, the wine does too – unless you trouble to tip "the tippling waiters" for the good stuff.

Review, with surveyors' comments in quotes

Restaurants with Top 50 Food rankings are in CAPITAL letters.

Before each review a symbol indicates whether responses were uniform ■ or mixed ◪.

Hours: ◑ serves after 11 PM, Ⓢ open on Sunday, Ⓛ serves lunch, Ⓜ open on Monday

Credit Cards: ⊄ no credit cards accepted

Ratings: Food, Decor and Service are rated on a scale of **0** to **30**. The Cost (C) column reflects our surveyors' estimate of the price of dinner including one drink and tip.

F	Food	D	Decor	S	Service	C	Cost
23		9		13		$15	

0–9	poor to fair	**20–25**	very good to excellent
10–15	fair to good	**26–30**	extraordinary to perfection
16–19	good to very good	▽	low response/less reliable

For places listed without ratings or a cost estimate, such as an important **newcomer** or a popular **write-in,** the cost is indicated by the following symbols.

I	$15 and below	**E**	$31 to $50
M	$16 to $30	**VE**	$51 or more

ALBION RIVER INN ⑤Ⓜ　　25　24　25　$46
3790 Shoreline Hwy./Hwy. 1 (Albion Airport Rd.), Albion, 707-937-1919

■ "Romance rules" at this "incomparable" address "overlooking the Pacific" that "blends a relaxed North Coast [character] with exquisite attention to detail"; it's a perennial "top pick in Mendocino County" thanks to "delightfully presented", "out-of-this-world" Cal fare and a "knowledgeable staff" that suggests "worthwhile pairings" from a wine list that's "heavy on the local good stuff"; "complete your meal with an amazing single malt from the endless list of scotch" and stay in one of the "luxury cabins."

Alexis Baking Company Ⓛ⑤Ⓜ　　20　11　13　$17
(aka ABC)
1517 Third St. (School St.), Napa, 707-258-1827

■ Co-chef/owner "Alexis Handelman holds court" at her "funky" bakery-oriented American cafe "in unpretentious Napa city proper"; "for what she does" – mostly "superb breakfasts", boxed lunches and "killer cakes" – "she does it well"; just "count on waiting" because it's an "institution" among "local winemakers and vineyard managers."

ALL SEASON'S CAFE AND WINE SHOP Ⓛ⑤Ⓜ　　23　18　23　$31
1400 Lincoln Ave. (Washington St.), Calistoga, 707-942-9111

■ "What could be better than browsing a well-stocked, fairly priced wine shop, walking two feet with your purchase and ordering great food to drink it with?" ask fans who frequent this "kooky but adorable" "diner-like" cafe "in the heart of Calistoga"; a "new chef" (a Thomas Keller protégé) whips up "great seasonal" Cal–New French fare that's deemed the "perfect après–mud bath meal."

APPLEWOOD INN & RESTAURANT　　24　23　25　$42
13555 Hwy. 116 (River Rd.), Guerneville, 707-869-9093

■ Boasting a "balcony overlooking a courtyard" and a "perfect setting" "right on the Russian River", this little-known, "very pink villa" sets a Californian–New French table that emphasizes "local ingredients and wines" (e.g. pork loin cured in house-pressed apple cider); since it's also a "nice place to stay", this "Guerneville treasure" is "easily worth the drive – and the calories."

AUBERGE DU SOLEIL L S M 26 | 27 | 25 | $66
Auberge du Soleil Inn, 180 Rutherford Hill Rd. (Silverado Trail), Rutherford, 707-967-3111
■ Dining at this "magnificent" Rutherford "romantic" is "like making it into heaven" – and not simply because it's got "one hell of a view" "overlooking the valley" and vineyards; chef Richard Reddington's "exquisite version of" French-Med cuisine "makes it nearly impossible to choose" and the international wine list (1,250 labels rich) "isn't bad either" – plus, there's "top-notch service" "to match"; although the place is "stiffly priced", the "view is the same, and much cheaper, at lunch."

Bistro at Glen Ellen L S M ∇ 15 | 15 | 13 | $31
13740 Arnold Dr. (Rte. 12), Glen Ellen, 707-996-4401
■ While ratings don't yet fully reflect it, "new chef" Brian Sinnott (ex mc^2) is "getting it right" with his Eclectic–New American cooking at this Glen Ellen eatery that offers a choice between a "charming creekside" patio seat or a "romantic table by the fireplace" inside; "reasonable prices" help "make it a good spot to end your day in Sonoma."

BISTRO
DON GIOVANNI L S M 24 | 22 | 22 | $40
4110 St. Helena Hwy./Hwy. 29 (bet. Oak Knoll & Salvador Aves.), Napa, 707-224-3300
■ Although its "non-pretentious Italian" menu is "not as exotic as the other famed restaurants'" in Napa, there's a reason why "wine industry" folk (don't be surprised to "see Robert Mondavi") and "smart locals" migrate to this "casual, festive" trattoria situated "among the vineyards": the "unparalleled pastas", the "excellent selection" of vino and "friendly service" all "guarantee a good time."

BISTRO JEANTY ● L S M | 26 | 21 | 23 | $43 |
6510 Washington St. (Mulberry St.), Yountville, 707-944-0103
■ Chef-owner Philippe Jeanty's "eponymous" eatery even "out-bistros Paris", because "it's friendlier" and you only have to drive to Yountville to savor it; "food purists" who "make regular pilgrimages" insist the combination of "luscious" "hearty fare" ("no nouvelle or diets here"), "charming" "rustic decor" and "unpretentious" ambiance (including a "fantastic community table") is "worth every decibel" and dollar – though actually the reasonable prices are pretty "*incroyable.*"

Bistro Ralph L M | 21 | 16 | 21 | $38 |
109 Plaza St. (Healdsburg Ave.), Healdsburg, 707-433-1380
■ After 10 years, palates still tingle at chef-owner Ralph's "lively" New American located "on the picturesque square in Healdsburg"; although the "limited menu" changes weekly, you can always count on the "same ole, same ole" "favorite chicken livers and great Liberty duck" confit and the "outstanding offering of Sonoma County" "wines by the glass"; drinkers deem "the bar seating" much better than the dining room's "cramped quarters."

Boonville Hotel S M   ▽ | 22 | 22 | 22 | $42 |
14050 Hwy. 128 (Lambert Ln.), Boonville, 707-895-2210
■ Situated in quirky Boonville, this upscale roadhouse is much more than a "terrific way station on a long drive" up the Mendocino coast; intrepid travelers insist the "creative" "often-changing" Cal–New American menu that "uses lots of fresh and local produce (mostly grown on the premises)" is "well worth the" commute, but nonetheless urge "spend the night" in the newly renovated Shaker-chic hotel.

BOUCHON ● L S M | 23 | 23 | 21 | $43 |
6534 Washington St. (Yount St.), Yountville, 707-944-8037
☑ "Another killer Thomas Keller winner" hail habitués of this "bustling" "Parisian bistro" that's an affordable "consolation prize" for "not getting into its sister French Laundry"; expect "fantastically authentic food" (think steak frites, blood

sausage), "stunning" Montparnasse decor (including sidewalk seating) and a "great wine selection (what else?)", but "bring your earplugs" and be prepared to "love thy neighbor because you'll be sitting in his lap"; happily, it "stays open late (not many in Napa Valley do)".

Brannan's Grill **L** **S** **M**　　18 | 21 | 19 | $33
1374 Lincoln Ave. (bet. Cedar & Washington Sts.), Calistoga, 707-942-2233

☑ A "well-done interior" "sets the tone" for this "fantastic Craftsman's" "Calistoga dining room" replete with "high-polish fern bar" and "big large booths"; its location "right in town" near the spas is a boon to "tourons" who can "enjoy that glass of wine" and New American fare "so much better knowing that bed is just steps away"; however, locals grouse about "wine-country prices" for the "nowhere-as-creative menu" since the departure of last year's chef.

Brix **L** **S**　　21 | 21 | 20 | $42
7377 St. Helena Hwy./Hwy. 29 (Washington St.), Napa, 707-944-2749

☑ Sojourners swoon that "the vineyard views", "strolls through the gardens" and "train chugging by at sunset all enhance a great dining experience" at this "elegant" Napa source for "creative" Cal cuisine with "an Asian influence" (slightly tweaked since ushering a "new chef") and a "well-done wine list"; however, skeptics sniff it's "somewhat inconsistent", warning with so "many other restaurants in the area", "they better tighten up on service."

CAFE BEAUJOLAIS **S** **M**　　25 | 19 | 23 | $48
961 Ukiah St. (School St.), Mendocino, 707-937-5614

■ This venerable "expensive-but-worth-it" dinner house "right in Downtown Mendocino" continues to maintain the "perfect" recipe "for a romantic weekend" – "quaint Victorian" charm and "creative" Californian-French "food that warms your soul in the cool, crisp [coastal] weather"; though "the founders have been gone for some time", "the homemade breads" and "same friendly servers" "are as unforgettable as ever", causing out-of-towners to sigh, "it's tragically unfair that [something] this good is so far away."

Cafe Citti ⬛🅂🅼　　　21 | 13 | 16 | $24
9049 Sonoma Hwy./Hwy. 12 (Shaw Ave.), Kenwood, 707-833-2690
■ Citti folk "would prefer to keep" this "roadside" trattoria in an "unassuming corner" of Kenwood "a secret but it's too late" – word has already seeped out that the "hearty" Northern Italian food at "reasonable prices" makes it a "great place for lunch when winery hopping" or a "casual dinner"; so "ignore the deli decor and dig into" "awesome rotisserie chicken and super Caesar salad."

CAFE LA HAYE 🅂　　　26 | 17 | 24 | $38
140 E. Napa St. (bet. 1st & 2nd Sts.), Sonoma, 707-935-5994
■ Say hey to this "tiny restaurant with an even tinier kitchen" whose "consistently" "well executed" regional New American fare "pays attention to freshness and flavor" while its "personable owner" pays attention to his guests; "coupled with a central location" and "excellent art shows", you'll see why it's considered "the pride of Sonoma" and why it's packed with locals and visitors "unwinding at the end of a long day of winery hopping."

CAFE LOLO ⬛🅼　　　25 | 17 | 21 | $39
620 Fifth St. (bet. D St. & Mendocino Ave.), Santa Rosa, 707-576-7822
■ This "Santa Rosa landmark hasn't been discovered by tourists, but locals love it" and are "rather glad" to keep the secret as "it's not very big" and enough folks already cram the "cozy" space for chef/co-owner Michael Quigley's "superb" American "gourmet comfort food"; "service is sometimes slow", but "terrific area wines" compensate.

Cafe Lucy Le Petit Bistro ⬛　　　▽ 24 | 12 | 20 | $23
1408 Clay St. (Jefferson St.), Napa, 707-255-0110
■ "What kept you guys so long in finding out about this gem?" marvel in-the-know Napans who "keep coming back" for the namesake chef-owner's "terrific" "eclectic

mix of" Cal-Provençale cuisines; true there are "no interior decorating statements here" (though you can "eat outside under the vines") – "just delicious, unpretentious" fare and a "courageously off-beat wine list", making it a great "getaway from the high-priced restaurants" of the area.

Cafe Prima **L** **S** **M**   ▽ | 18 | 19 | 15 | $28 |

124 E. Laurel St. (bet. Franklin & Main Sts.), Fort Bragg, 707-964-0563

◪ The Ivory Coast meets the North Coast at this "unusual" African where the eats are "different without being weird"; the few intrepid travelers who've discovered it declare Kenyan-born chef Raymond Thoya "is a magician" at "co-mingling the foods of his native country" with the "Cal cuisine" sensibility of Fort Bragg ("the samosas are worth their weight in ivory"); however, complaints surface about "inconsistent service" and hours.

Calistoga Inn
Restaurant & Brewery **L** **S** **M** | 18 | 19 | 18 | $34 |

1250 Lincoln Ave. (Cedar St.), Calistoga, 707-942-4101

■ "Conveniently located on Calistoga's main drag", this "budget-minded" brewery offers a laid-back spot to "lounge on the large patio by" the Napa River to "listen to live music and enjoy a house brew" (that is, if "you can still drink after all that wine tasting") and "generally good" American fare grilled over a wood-fired barbecue.

Carneros **L** **S** **M**   ▽ | 22 | 19 | 18 | $40 |

The Lodge at Sonoma, 1325 Broadway (Leveroni Rd.), Sonoma, 707-931-2042

■ "All hotel eating should be this good" crow Carneros-vores after sampling the "absolutely delicious", "finely crafted menu" at The Lodge at Sonoma; the Cal-Med menu employs only regional cheeses, breads and produce, and the 100 percent Sonoma wine list (heavily weighted with in-house bottlings) is "one of the most educational you'll see"; "cool local art" and "excellent service" round out a most "enjoyable" experience.

Catahoula　　　　　　　21 | 18 | 20 | $39
Restaurant & Saloon Ⓛ Ⓢ Ⓜ

Mount View Hotel, 1457 Lincoln Ave. (bet. Fair Way &
Washington St.), Calistoga, 707-942-2275

■ "Big Daddy" "Jan Birnbaum is still knocking 'em dead
with his" "down-home Southern cooking" ("tasty rooster
gumbo", "soft, sexy grits") at this "lively" "casual" Calistoga
hangout that's packed with "locals and tourists alike"; it's
"not for dieters", but the "adventurous" say "it's a nice
change of cuisine" (even if it does – horrors – "require
beer in the heart of the wine country").

CELADON Ⓛ Ⓜ　　　　　23 | 18 | 20 | $35

1040 Main St. (bet. 1st & Pearl Sts.), Napa, 707-254-9690
■ "You'll have to search for the entry to [owner] Greg
Cole's hideaway", but fans insist the "consistently tasty"
"imaginative" Med–New American menu is "worth the
trouble"; the "intimate surroundings" make for a "cozy
atmosphere" but the "ambiance is best when you can sit
outside"; Napa natives are green with envy that the crowd is
"now mostly non-locals"; N.B. it was scheduled to move
to the Napa Mill complex (500 Main Street) at press time.

Charcuterie Ⓛ Ⓢ Ⓜ　　　20 | 14 | 17 | $33

335 Healdsburg Ave. (Plaza St.), Healdsburg, 707-431-7213
■ There are "pigs, pigs everywhere" but not a drop to eat
(save the signature pork tenderloin) at this wee wee wee
Healdsburg cafe that once was "a real charcuterie" but now
is simply an "unpretentious, but satisfying" "Cal-French
bistro" with "reasonable prices" and "lighthearted service";
while the "whimsical" "porcine-themed decor" offers
"tons to look at", surveyors snort "it's not exactly pretty."

CHATEAU SOUVERAIN CAFÉ　22 | 26 | 21 | $45
AT THE WINERY Ⓛ Ⓢ Ⓜ

400 Souverain Rd. (Hwy. 101, Independence Ln. exit),
Geyserville, 707-433-3141
☑ You might "go for the wine" but you'll "stay for the Cal-
French food" say smitten surveyors about this "gorgeous"

winery restaurant "set among the vineyards" in Geyserville; "when you drive up you feel like you're going to eat at a palace" and the service keeps up the illusion, though perhaps it is "a bit arch" for some tastes, which also note the cuisine is not "as perfect as the surroundings"; still, it's ideal "for a summer lunch", served alfresco until 5 PM.

COLE'S CHOP HOUSE 🆂 Ⓜ

| 21 | 21 | 21 | $49 |

1122 Main St. (bet. 1st & Pearl Sts.), Napa, 707-224-6328

☑ "Chicago meets Napa" at this "two-tier" steakhouse offering the "absolute best red-meat fix in the valley"; while the "dry-aged steaks are to die for", they're "priced as if they were in Manhattan", a downer "considering you have to order the sides" separately; while the house remains "lively" and "crowded", a drop in the ratings across the board suggests that it might be losing some of its chops.

Costeaux Bakery and Cafe 🅻🆂Ⓜ

▽ | 20 | 14 | 14 | $14 |

417 Healdsburg Ave. (bet. North & Piper Sts.), Healdsburg, 707-433-1913

■ This "fabulous" family-owned and operated "working bakery" (since 1923) is "good to drop into for coffee", "out-of-this-world pastries" and "fantastic" "French onion soup"; alternatively, you can get boxed "sandwiches for picnics" featuring their signature sourdough breads before heading through Healdsburg and points north; N.B. closes at 5 PM.

Cucina Paradiso 🅻🆂Ⓜ

▽ | 25 | 17 | 24 | $31 |

Golden Eagle Shopping Ctr., 56 E. Washington St. (Petaluma Blvd.), Petaluma, 707-782-1130

■ The rather nondescript "strip mall location" of this "authentic little trattoria" belies the "finesse and the light hand" of its *cucina*; armed with "a good selection of Californian and Italian wines" and "attentive staff", it's considered "one of the better places in the North Bay" by locals, and while "the decor ain't everything", "eating alfresco on warm nights" is as close to paradise in Petaluma as you're gonna get.

Cucina Viansa 🅛🅢🅜   ▽ 17 | 17 | 13 | $25 |

Sonoma Plaza, 400 First St. E. (Spain St.), Sonoma, 707-935-5656

■ Situated right on the Sonoma Plaza, this "very casual" Northern Italian is "a great place to stop for a sandwich or nice salad" in your travels around the wine country; but the bar is also primo for tasting the bottlings of its parent Viansa Winery, particularly on Friday and Saturday nights when you can sip and be serenaded by a rotating variety of live music.

Della Santina's 🅛🅢🅜   20 | 19 | 19 | $33 |

133 E. Napa St. (1st St.), Sonoma, 707-935-0576

■ Although it's located "right off the square" in Sonoma, "dinner in the garden on a sunny day" "transports you back to Italy" at this stalwart; "there's no pretense in the menu – just food like mama makes", if you were lucky enough to grow up "in Lucca" (think rotisseried rabbits and the "best gnocchi you've ever had"); "cozy atmosphere" and a "really wonderful staff" round out the appeal.

Deuce 🅛🅢🅜   ▽ 20 | 17 | 20 | $36 |

691 Broadway (Andrieux St.), Sonoma, 707-933-3823

■ "It's worth going a few blocks off the Sonoma square" to find this "family-owned" 1890 house sporting a "charming" "patio for alfresco dining"; but don't let the "old-fashioned ambiance" fool you – the Deuce's wild yet "excellently prepared" New American menu is 21st-century "hip" (specials include "anything from ostrich to alligator"), with a "great wine list" from the county to accompany it.

DOMAINE CHANDON 🅛🅢   26 | 26 | 25 | $58 |

1 California Dr. (Hwy. 29), Yountville, 707-944-2892

■ There isn't a better "spot to go broke" than this "magical" Yountville winery restaurant situated "only a few stumbles from an outstanding champagne cellar"; visitors can tour the facility "and then sit down" "in the lap of luxury" to "absolutely fantastic" New French–Cal cuisine, proffered by "attentive and discreet" servers; those who want their kick without the hangover-inducing prices can sit on the "patio looking over the well-manicured grounds" and opt for the "sparkling-wine sampler" and appetizers.

DOWNTOWN   25 | 11 | 17 | $13
BAKERY & CREAMERY 🅛🅢🅜⊘
308A Center St. (Matheson St.), Healdsburg, 707-431-2719
■ "Who needs Krispy Kreme" when you can load up on the "amazing sticky buns, homemade ice-cream sandwiches" and delectable "little pizza breads" at this "old-timey" bakery in Healdsburg; it's "strictly takeaway", so "sit on the bench out front and meet the locals and their dogs."

DRY CREEK KITCHEN 🅛🅢🅜   24 | 26 | 20 | $56
Hotel Healdsburg, 317 Healdsburg Ave. (Matheson St.), Healdsburg, 707-431-0330
◪ "Manhattan comes to Healdsburg in the best way" thanks to "the new star of Sonoma, Charlie Palmer" who "courts the upscale crowd" with a "chic" decor, an all-local "wine list that could take you days to" read and "wonderfully prepared seasonal and regional food" in his New American kitchen; most welcome every aspect of the New York state of mind "except for the 'tude" of the staff, which is "almost too sophisticated for laid-back wine country"; P.S. "BYO" indigenous vintages "and they waive the corkage fee."

Duck Club 🅢🅜   20 | 21 | 20 | $43
Bodega Bay Lodge & Spa, 103 Coast Hwy. 1 (Doran Beach Rd.), Bodega, 707-875-3525
◪ "The older crowd tends to enjoy this" hotel eatery for – what else? – "to-die-for-duck" and other "elegant New American eats" served in a "tranquil setting" (nary a "hint of duck blinds", but "lovely ocean views"); "for what it is and where it is", it's "a solid choice", even if critics quack "you can do better for the price."

Farmhouse Inn & Restaurant, The 🇸　　▽ 22 | 21 | 23 | $41

Farmhouse Inn, 7871 River Rd. (Wohler Rd.), Forestville, 707-887-3300

■ This "wonderful" Forestville inn, located off the back roads of Sonoma's Russian River Valley, is turning heads since new owners revamped the "restored country home"; while the same chefs are cranking out "sublime" Cal wine-country–inspired fare (like the signature 'rabbit, rabbit, rabbit', in which the lowly hare is prepared three ways), the newfound "superb service" and "excellent", souped-up wine list have diners "sorry we waited so long to try" it.

FEAST 🇱🇲　　　　　　22 | 23 | 21 | $40

714 Village Ct. (bet. Claremont Dr. & Patio Ct.), Santa Rosa, 707-591-9800

■ "What [a difference] a new location" makes fawn fans as they feast their eyes on the "larger", more "comfy" and "contemporary" digs of this New American now located in Santa Rosa's Monterey Village (making it a "popular ladies-who-lunch spot"); a few folks feel "they need to grow into this new space", but chef/co-owner Jesse McQuarrie's "creative cooking" "ranks up there as one of SoCo's best."

Felix & Louie's 🇸🇲　　　　14 | 17 | 16 | $32

106 Matheson St. (Healdsburg Ave.), Healdsburg, 707-433-6966

☑ Often "noisily" filled with the "overflow" from sister Bistro Ralph, this "fun" "casual" spot is one of the best joints in Healdsburg to "drop in for a drink" and hear "great jazz" ("every Wednesday and Sunday") in the "huge bar area"; however, despite its "prices and pedigree", the American-Italian menu is "inconsistent" ("wood-fired pizza is your best bet") and the "service needs serious reconstruction."

Flatiron Grill 🇸🇲　　　　– | – | – | M

1440 Lincoln Ave. (bet. Fair Way & Washington St.), Calistoga, 707-942-1220

Brought to you by the Brannan's folks, this "reasonably priced" Calistoga newcomer's already "a hit with locals" who fill the "beautiful" booths; oil paintings of grazing cows bedeck the walls, and meat dishes abound on the American menu, from the namesake steak to dry-rubbed babyback ribs.

FOOTHILL CAFE ⑤ 24 | 14 | 18 | $37

J&P Shopping Ctr., 2766 Old Sonoma Rd. (Foothill Blvd.), Napa, 707-252-6178
■ Only in the wine country would folks refer to a place as "your typical neighborhood strip-mall gourmet restaurant"; "don't let the location deter you" from chowing down on "finger-licking ribs" and "wonderful" Cal fare; even if it is a "great-kept secret" among insiders, it's still mighty "loud and crowded" with Napans who know a "good value."

FRENCH LAUNDRY Ⓛ⑤Ⓜ 29 | 26 | 28 | $100

6640 Washington St. (Creek St.), Yountville, 707-944-2380
■ "Gaining a table has become a badge of courage" at Yountville's New American–French "epicurean cathedral" – but "everything you've heard is true": "Thomas Keller should have his hands bronzed" for the "culinary pyrotechnics" that produce his "ethereal", "inventive" and "humorous" tasting menus (both meat and veggie) in a "sublime setting"; even with "seamless service", you must "plan on three hours" and expect "obscene prices", but every foodie "should indulge" "before he dies."

GARY CHU Ⓛ⑤ 23 | 19 | 21 | $26

611 Fifth St. (bet. D & Mendocino Sts.), Santa Rosa, 707-526-5840
☑ "Santa Rosa isn't known for its Chinese food" but this eatery's eponymous restaurateur-around-town (he also owns Osake) woks up "Asian fare with a twist and zest" in an "upscale" yet "friendly" setting; but while it's the "best in the county", critical cosmopolites carp "it would be considered second-tier by SF standards."

General's Daughter, The Ⓛ⑤Ⓜ 19 | 24 | 20 | $40

400 W. Spain St. (4th St.), Sonoma, 707-938-4004
☑ "The general himself [Vallejo, that is] would enjoy the experience" afforded at his daughter's "historic" "Victorian

home", converted into a "charming" spot for "special-occasion" evenings or sunshiney "brunches alfresco"; the "rustic Californian cuisine" is "mostly good, but" "not good enough for the price" attack antagonists; still, "Sonoma locals love this place" and visitors can enjoy boutique "wines that you [often] cannot buy outside the area."

Geyserville Smokehouse, The 🄻🅂🄼   ▽ 21 | 18 | 19 | $22

21021 Geyserville Ave. (Hwy. 128), Geyserville, 707-857-4600

■ Smoking some of the "best ribs and brisket in Sonoma County", this year-old "mid-priced" "true locals'" BBQ "joint" in sleepy Geyserville is a "sorely needed" cure for an area overrun with "haughty" wine country establishments; "despite its newness, the fabulously restored antique building" decorated with Old West bric-a-brac "offers wonderful character and atmosphere."

girl & the fig, the 🄻🅂🄼   21 | 19 | 20 | $40

110 W. Spain St. (1st St.), Sonoma, 707-938-3634

■ Owner Sondra Bernstein "knows what she's doing" at her "whimsical gourmand fantasy" on the Sonoma square where "innovative" yet "solid country French" dishes and fancy "flights of wine" from an "eclectic list" are served in a "cozy" dining room graced with "eye-catching art" or an "inviting patio"; "friendly" service and a delightfully "low snobbery appeal" help make it a "popular spot with locals and tourists alike."

girl & the gaucho, the 🅂🄼   ▽ 23 | 18 | 20 | $39

13690 Arnold Dr. (O'Donnell Ln.), Glen Ellen, 707-938-2130

■ A gaggle of gauchos goes gaga over the "small plates with big flavors" and Southern Hemisphere wine flights at this slice of South America "in the Glen Ellen countryside", where you can have "something fabulous" that "won't break your bank"; although a few fashionistas fume owner "Sondra [Bernstein] has gone to one too many garage sales", most feel the "fun" funky decor (with a "velvet bull fighter on the wall") "works."

Glen Ellen Inn Restaurant 🇸Ⓜ ▽ 22 | 22 | 21 | $44
13670 Arnold Dr. (Warm Springs Rd.), Glen Ellen, 707-996-6409
■ "Fine dining and romance" await at this "charming" Glen Ellen Californian where "civilized evenings" can last "overnight" in the luxury creekside cottages; "wonderful" (if not "overly fussy") Golden State fare (including dayboat scallop BLTs and "homemade ice cream") and "great local wines" are served in a "lovely setting" (especially "outdoors in the summer") by a "superb" staff; N.B. now offering lunch Friday–Tuesday.

Gordon's 🇱🇸 ▽ 22 | 16 | 15 | $25
6770 Washington St. (Madison St.), Yountville, 707-944-8246
■ Early birds scramble for "big yummy breakfasts" and local vintners "gather around the long center table for lunch and conversation" at Sally Gordon's Yountville American; most of the week it's a counter-service affair offering "incredibly reasonable" morning and midday fare, but on Fridays nights, "excellent" "special" dinners (including an "amazing selection" of Napa wines at wholesale prices) are served in a room that's "completely transformed."

Graziano's Ristorante 🇸⇗ ▽ 24 | 21 | 21 | $35
170 Petaluma Blvd. N. (Washington St.), Petaluma, 707-762-5997
■ "Wonderful" chef-owner Graziano Perozzi "knows how to cook" "delicious, classic Italian" dishes in the "open kitchen" of his popular ristorante housed in Petaluma's historic Wickersham Building; the "congenial atmosphere" extends to "waiters who remember loyal patrons" and while the room "may be a little loud for most", amici say *grazie,* "it's nice to have an upbeat place in this sleepy town", even if it's a bit "pricey."

Green Valley Cafe 🇱 ▽ 21 | 12 | 19 | $25
1310 Main St. (Hunt Ave.), St. Helena, 707-963-7088
■ St. Helenans "hesitate to give away the secret" of this "terrific", "family-owned" Northern Italian specialist "favored by locals" for more than 10 years, serving "freshly

prepared", "simple", "*delicioso*" pastas, soups and other hearty grub in a "casual", "friendly" atmosphere that's rare for an area "full of attitude."

HANA JAPANESE ⬛🅂   26 | 14 | 19 | $38 |
Doubletree Plaza, 101 Golf Course Dr. (Roberts Lake Rd.), Rohnert Park, 707-586-0270
■ "*Kampai!*" cheer champions of this flower "in the middle of a strip mall" near Santa Rosa serving some of the "best Japanese fare north of the Golden Gate", including specials such as the *unagi*-and-foie-gras *nigiri* that "rivals any fancy restaurant in SF", as well as an "extensive sake list"; chef-owner Ken Tominaga is "truly dedicated to delighting customers", so cognoscenti counsel "just put yourself in his hands and be prepared to smile."

Jimtown Store ⬛🅂🅼   20 | 16 | 13 | $15 |
6706 Hwy. 128 (1 mi. east of Russian River), Healdsburg, 707-433-1212
■ This "kitschy" old general store/deli "is not to be missed when" winery-hopping in the Alexander Valley; most travelers "stop [in] for a snack" or takeout from their array of "creative sandwiches and addictive spreads", although there are "outdoor tables" which are "especially fun" in "good weather"; toss in "nice wines by the glass, fabulous retro merchandising" and "views of vineyards" and "what else could you want in a country store?"; N.B. no dinners.

JOHN ASH & CO. ⬛🅂🅼   24 | 25 | 23 | $49 |
Vintners Inn, 4330 Barnes Rd. (River Rd.), Santa Rosa, 707-527-7687
■ While this Santa Rosa stalwart is "off the highway", it feels like a "little find off a back road in Provence", thanks in part to the "killer setting" overlooking "the vineyards that probably grew the grapes for that glass of wine"; the kitchen "continues to offer some of the best Cal cuisine", plus "impeccable service"; while the dining rooms are "a bit more formal" than other Valley spots, it's "a good place to impress" – just be sure to "dust off your credit card."

JULIA'S KITCHEN ⬛Ⓛ Ⓢ Ⓜ　　25 | 15 | 21 | $44

COPIA, 500 First St. (Soscol Ave.), Napa, 707-265-5700

■ Living up to Julia Child's name is a tall order, but chef Mark Dommen rises to the challenge, creating a dynamic collection of "deftly balanced", "refined Cal-French" dishes (utilizing organic produce) in the "open kitchen" at this newcomer in Napa's COPIA Center; an all-American wine list, tended by an "excellent staff", complements the cuisine, served in an "austere", "modern" room; N.B. both the restaurant and its take-out sibling, the Market Cafe, can be accessed without paying the museum entrance fee.

K&L Bistro ⬛Ⓛ Ⓢ　　∇ 24 | 19 | 22 | $37

119 S. Main St. (Bodega Hwy./Hwy. 12), Sebastopol, 707-823-6614

■ Chef-spouses Karin and Lucas Martin's (ex SF's Hayes Street Grill) "more-than-wonderful addition to the local food scene" brings "a touch of France to the heart of Sebastopol"; in the open-kitchen of their "charming", "intimate" bistro, the couple whips up "outstanding" boudin blanc sausages, addictive frites and other Gallic goodies on a daily changing menu.

KENWOOD ⬛Ⓛ Ⓢ　　24 | 21 | 22 | $41

9900 Sonoma Hwy./Hwy. 12 (Warm Springs Rd.), Kenwood, 707-833-6326

■ "What a find on Highway 12!" gush wine country travelers who stumble upon this "roadside retreat" in Kenwood where chef-owner Max Schacher's "well-crafted and -presented" "fine French-American" dishes are served in a charming room graced with "vibrant paintings" and a patio "nestled among the vineyards"; "unintrusive, professional service" is another reason why it's a "wonderful alternative to all the trendy places" in Sonoma.

LaSalette Ⓢ　　∇ 29 | 18 | 24 | $35

18625 Sonoma Hwy. (Siesta Way), Sonoma, 707-938-1927

■ The "best of Portugal" awaits at chef-owner Manuel Azevedo's "cozy" cottage off the Sonoma Highway, serving his "lovingly prepared", "fantastic" dishes and "interesting Portuguese wines" that are recommended by the "attentive" staff "to complement the food, not to please the wine salesman"; N.B. Fado Nights on the third Friday of every month feature live traditional folk music and a set menu.

LA TOQUE 🖪   27 | 25 | 26 | $80

1140 Rutherford Rd. (Hwy. 29), Rutherford, 707-963-9770

■ "These people know what they're doing, in the kitchen, at the table, in the cellar" at Ken Frank's "romantic" Rutherford affair exclaim enthusiasts enraptured by "absolutely dazzling" "multiple-course prix fixes" of "fantastic" French fare enhanced by "creative combinations and terrific sauces" and "inspired wine pairings" suggested by the "exceptional" staff; so "why hold for French Laundry" when it's "so much easier to get into" this spot, "one of the must-stops in the Napa Valley"?

Lauren's ⊘   ▽ 20 | 13 | 21 | $27

14211 Hwy. 128 (across from fairgrounds), Boonville, 707-895-3869

■ For a "real Mendocino County experience" or a "break" "on your way from driving" through Anderson Valley, cognoscenti recommend this "typically Boonville funky" spot for its American-International "home-style cooking" that's "better than your mother's" and "friendly", "casual" atmosphere; chances are you'll find it packed with "locals (including [owner] Lauren Keating)" "enjoying themselves."

LEDFORD HOUSE 🖪   22 | 22 | 23 | $45

3000 Shoreline Hwy./Hwy. 1 (Spring Grove Rd.), Albion, 707-937-0282

■ "Wonderful" service, a "splendid setting" "overlooking the blue Pacific" ("get there before sundown") and an "artfully prepared" "North Coast meets the South of France" menu have made this Cal-Med one of the "Mendocino coast's favorites" "for a romantic dinner" since 1987; there's "live jazz every night" and on Sundays "a three-course 'supper club special' that's a terrific value."

LISA HEMENWAY'S BISTRO 🄻🄼   22 | 19 | 23 | $37

*Town & Country Shopping Ctr., 1612 Terrace Way
(Town & Country Dr.), Santa Rosa, 707-526-5111*

◪ Run by a "locally famous chef with some unique ideas",
this Asian–New French gets "an uneven dining report card"
from Santa Rosa patrons; friends find "everything here is
letter-perfect", from "the quote painted on the beams" to its
"well-executed menu" to the "staff that makes strangers
feel [as] welcome as regulars"; but tough graders say the
fare is "just not as creative or consistent" "as it once was."

Little River Inn 🅂🄼   21 | 21 | 22 | $35

*Little River Inn, 7901 Shoreline Hwy./Hwy. 1
(Little River Airport Rd.), Little River, 707-937-5942*

■ After a day of golf or tooling around Mendocino village,
head to this "romantic" resort where "chef Silver Canul's
Mexican roots add a touch of innovation and spice" to the
Californian menu served in the "lovely dining room that
overlooks an immaculate garden"; weekend "brunches
are just as wonderful", though some prefer "pulling up a
stool" at the Ole's Whale Watch bar, which has a "less
pricey menu" and a "beautiful view of the surf."

Lucy's Restaurant, Bar & Bakery 🄻🅂🄼   ▽ 18 | 18 | 15 | $24

*6948 Sebastopol Ave. (bet. Main St. & Petaluma Ave.),
Sebastopol, 707-829-9713*

◪ It boasts a "new location", new chef and newly added
bar, but this Sebastopol standby is still the same Cal-Med
hippie hangout, serving "breads baked on the premises"
and "excellent pizzas with ingredients from the [organic]
garden"; however, some snipe "they're still getting used to"
things ("service is a little shaky and the kitchen timing is off").

MACCALLUM HOUSE 🅂🄼   23 | 23 | 23 | $38

*MacCallum House Inn, 45020 Albion St. (Lansing St.),
Mendocino, 707-937-5763*

■ Both "hungers and moods are wonderfully satisfied" at
"the 'MacHouse'", a historic "seaside home" turned B&B

in Mendocino village; "chef-owner Alan Kantor is nuts about choosing the penultimate purveyor" for his "North Coast cuisine", served by a "very friendly staff"; while "you can dine in the old Victorian rooms and gaze at the Bay or the garden", "locals belly up to the bar" where they "lay on a humpback sofa and have their lovers feed them succulent" yet "cheaper" fare.

MADRONA MANOR S M 25 | 25 | 24 | $55
Madrona Manor Wine Country Inn, 1001 Westside Rd. (W. Dry Creek Rd.), Healdsburg, 707-433-4231
■ The most "manorly" of experiences can be had at this 1881 "grand Victorian" mansion outside Healdsburg: from chef Jesse Malgren's (ex Stars) "exquisite" Californian-French fare (employing ingredients plucked from the grounds' garden) to the "exceptional" staff holding forth in a series of "homely elegant" candlelit rooms, everything is "impeccable across the board"; P.S. "if possible, plan to stay overnight at the beautiful inn."

MANZANITA S 23 | 18 | 21 | $43
336 Healdsburg Ave. (North St.), Healdsburg, 707-433-8111
◪ At this Healdsburg haven, stacks of Manzanita timber tip you off that the "best items" on the "constantly changing and clever Med menu" are from the "wood-fired oven" that dominates the room ("the flatbread in particular inspires severe cravings"); the addition of a "world-class savvy wine list" ("one of the few in Sonoma that has great European" vintages) causes most to call this freshman a "wonderful find", but frigid types find the "decor cold" and everything else "overhyped" and "overrated."

Marché aux Fleurs L ▽ 24 | 17 | 23 | $45
23 Ross Common (off Lagunitas Rd.), Ross, 415-925-9200
■ For "a little Provence in little Ross", Peter Mayle fans march over to this "delightful" "hideaway" known for its "spectacular New French food" meted out by "attentive servers who know your name" and an "affordable wine

list focusing on family vineyards" that "you'll never be able to find again"; perhaps "portions are relatively" petit, but all's forgiven "sitting on the wonderful patio" "perfectly placed under the trees."

MARTINI HOUSE L S M   24 | 26 | 22 | $51 |
1245 Spring St. (bet. Hwy. 29/Main & Oak Sts.), St. Helena, 707-963-2233

■ Co-owner "Pat Kuleto does it again" at this "converted Craftsman house"; boasting a "cozy river-rock fireplace", "the downstairs bar is *the* happening scene in St. Helena" but the entire "rustic" setting is "an appropriate showcase" for executive chef Todd Humphries (ex SF's Campton Place), who presents "thoughtful", "inventive" New American dishes of locally foraged ingredients; they're accompanied by "an awesome wine list" featuring both international vintages and regional heavy-hitters.

Maya L S M   ▽ 18 | 19 | 15 | $26 |
101 E. Napa St. (1st St. E.), Sonoma, 707-935-3500

■ This "upscale Mexican" located in a 150-year-old stone building "close to the Sonoma square" offers Yucatan-style dinners that "make good use of spices and fruit"; however, what really gets surveyors to shout are the offerings made at the Temple of Tequila bar, including the "yum yum" house lemonade and the "best fresh-squeezed" "hand-shaken margaritas" "in town."

Meadowood Grill L S M   21 | 22 | 23 | $44 |
Meadowood Resort, 900 Meadowood Ln. (Howell Mountain Rd., off Silverado Trail), St. Helena, 707-963-3646

◪ "Located in the plush Meadowood Country Club", this Californian's "view from the terrace" "overlooking the croquet field", paired with "professional service", "puts you in such a state that they could serve cold hot dogs and it would be a great meal"; happily, "the "food is much better than that" and though some sniff "it's not quite worth the dollar", the wine list (strong in Napa Valley bottlings) helps ensure a "relaxing atmosphere."

Mendo Bistro ⑤Ⓜ 21 17 19 $29
301 N. Main St. (Redwood St.), Fort Bragg, 707-964-4974
■ Chef-owner Nicolas Petty may don a "jester cap" "but he's dead serious about his" "sophisticated" Med–New American cooking that's "better than most on the North Coast at a fraction of the price"; the interactive menu lets you "pick your main course, its preparation and sauce" (definitely start with his "award-winning crab cakes" though); despite being located "on the mezzanine of the Old Company Store", the food, along with the "dedicated, loyal staff" make it worth the drive to Fort Bragg.

Miramonte 19 19 19 $38
Restaurant & Café Ⓛ⑤Ⓜ
1327 Railroad Ave. (bet. Adams & Hunt Sts.), St. Helena, 707-963-1200
◪ "If you like foods of the Americas" (anything from fish tostadas to duck burgers) then "you'll love" owner Cindy Pawlcyn's (of Mustards Grill) yearling that whips up "a creative mix of fare" along with "exotic cocktails" and "Mexican wines from Baja" in a "bright", "contemporary" (some say "stark") interior; but while amigos appreciate this "refreshing change" in the all-"too-touristy mecca" of St. Helena, enimigos find it "disappointingly" "inconsistent."

Mirepoix – – – E
275 Windsor River Rd. (Bell Rd.), Windsor, 707-838-0162
In Mariposa's old place, this New French–New American newcomer seems "definitely worth a trip" to Windsor say early birds who've found it; such "imaginative" specialties as arctic char with mushrooms, served in a room with floor-to-ceiling windows or on the seasonal patio, make for a most "enjoyable" experience.

MIXX RESTAURANT Ⓛ Ⓜ 22 19 22 $37
Historic Railroad Sq., 135 Fourth St. (Davis St.), Santa Rosa, 707-573-1344
◪ This Santa Rosa stalwart "in Railroad Square" "used to be Sonoma County's hot spot" and its "beautiful" "roomy"

"old-fashioned bar" *the* "meeting place to wine and dine" (thanks to a "nice vino list featuring local producers"); while many feel the Californian "food is still good", especially if you "trust the staff's recommendations", trendoids mixx things up by dissing the "rude service" and declaring the place "is played out."

Model Bakery L S ▽ 24 | 15 | 17 | $12

1357 Main St. (bet. Adams & Spring Sts.), St. Helena, 707-963-8192

■ Sporting a "vintage interior", this St. Helena bakery whips up "the yummiest way to start the day in Napa Valley" – namely "disgustingly good pastries and coffees" to be consumed at communal tables; locals are equally sweet on the "super soups" and wood-fired oven-baked pizzas that round out the day's offerings; N.B. closes at 6 PM.

MOOSSE CAFE L S M 22 | 16 | 18 | $33

Blue Heron Inn, 390 Kasten St. (Albion St.), Mendocino, 707-937-4323

◪ "In an area with a lot of good food", this Mendocino Californian "set in a redone Victorian [house] with a tiny inn upstairs" and a stunning "garden with ocean view" "stands out for its coziness, creativity and deliciousness"; the space is "unfortunately small" and "scrunched" "for such large flavors"; "however, the staff is lovely."

MUSTARDS GRILL L S M 23 | 18 | 20 | $39

7399 St. Helena Hwy./Hwy. 29 (Yountville Rd.), Napa, 707-944-2424

■ Cindy Pawlcyn's "wine country roadhouse" "broke new ground when it opened" in 1983 and today it still cuts the mustard; her "innovative twists on" New American fare ("with Asian influences") coupled with "knowledgeable servers" (especially "helpful" with the "huge wine list") "make for a fun escapade"; since it lacks Napa's usual "atmospheric prices", it's perennially packed, but you can always have "a quick bite at the bar among local winemakers" ("we sat next to the Mondavis").

Napa Valley Grille L S M   19 | 18 | 19 | $37
Washington Sq., 6795 Washington St. (Madison St.), Yountville, 707-944-8686

☑ This Yountville chain link has staked a claim with "filling portions" of Californian fare and "easygoing" ambiance that's a "pleasant, less expensive alternative to the high-priced" Napa eateries; however, while the "all-day menu" and "nice patio" offer a good "bet for lunch", foes find "staff changes in the back of the house" "have made the food inconsistent" (as reflected by a drop in the score), and ask "why waste a night [here] with so many better alternatives?"

Napa Valley Wine Train L S M   16 | 22 | 19 | $60
1275 McKinstry St. (bet. 1st St. & Soscol Ave.), Napa, 800-427-4124

☑ "Even "though it's touristy", this three-hour excursion on a historic locomotive "through the Napa Valley" is "a wonderful way to spend the afternoon" with "visiting relatives" (especially recommended: "the fun wine-tasting car"); still, some feel taken for a ride by the "standard" Cal cuisine and "premium prices", cracking "clickety-clack, won't go back"; N.B. there's now a package that includes lunch at the Domaine Chandon winery.

955 UKIAH S M   22 | 18 | 20 | $36
955 Ukiah St. (Lansing St.), Mendocino, 707-937-1955

☑ Artsy advocates adore the atelier-like interior "filled with paintings" of this homespun "establishment in Mendocino village", which specializes in "wonderfully" "innovative" New American–New French fare plucked from "local specialty produce"; dissenters dismiss it as an "overgrown natural foods cafe", but scores side with supporters who say this "charming" "obscure venue" is well "worth the path placed before you" to reach it.

Osake L M   ▽ 24 | 18 | 20 | $39
2446 Patio Ct. (Farmer's Ln.), Santa Rosa, 707-542-8282

■ "Sitting at the sushi bar" at this Santa Rosa Cal-Japanese is "like walking into Cheers with fish instead of beer" being proffered; indeed chef-owner Gary Chu "knows everyone's" name and everyone seems to adore his "very eclectic menu", which features both "nice new-wave rolls" and cooked seafood; "the huge fish tank at the entrance is beautiful", even if "it's a bit unnerving looking at the live version of what's on my plate."

Pairs L S M ▽ 16 | 14 | 15 | $35
4175 Solano Ave. (Wine Country Ave.), Napa, 707-224-8464
☑ Up Valley residents had high hopes for this Cal-"Asian fusion" joint that moved in 2001 to this "rather mundane" mini strip mall in the town of Napa; while many newcomers find the "educated cuisine" (replete with suggested wine pairings), "tacky sake" drinks and "enchanting" patio "exceed expectations", old-timers opine it's still "a little rough around the edges", declaring the food and service "were better in the old location in St. Helena."

Pangaea S ▽ 27 | 21 | 24 | $44
250 Main St. (Eureka Hill Rd.), Point Arena, 707-882-3001
■ "You'll be amazed at the extremely creative and expertly prepared fare" at this "inviting" restaurant "in the middle of nowhere" (aka Point Arena); the husband-and-wife owners whip up "zaftig flavors in an ever-changing menu" "that covers the globe" and a "carefully selected wine list" that features organic bottlings from around the world; while fans warn it's "not traditional", it's "maybe the best food" and "most fun on the North Coast."

Pearl L ▽ 22 | 15 | 21 | $30
1339 Pearl St. (bet. Franklin & Polk Sts.), Napa, 707-224-9161
■ This pearl of a place and "its enticing patio" is prized for chef/co-owner Nicki Zeller's "excellent Cal homestyle cooking, casual atmosphere and skillful service" ("with a reasonably priced wine list to boot"); savvy locals say go now, because "as the neighborhood around it undergoes a long-overdue facelift", it won't be Downtown Napa's "best-kept secret anymore."

Pho Vietnam ⬛🅻🅂🅼 ▽ 24 6 15 $10
711 Stony Point Rd. (Sebastopol Rd.), Santa Rosa, 707-571-7687
◪ Santa Rosa's "awesome" Vietnamese "is the hole-in-the-wall you always wish to find"; it's the "fragrant", "super-cheap" "bowls of noodle soup" "that the people come for", which more than "balance out" the "sometimes preoccupied staff" and pho-gettable "storefront decor."

Piatti 🅻🅂🅼 17 17 17 $33
El Dorado Hotel, 405 First St. W. (Spain St.), Sonoma, 707-996-2351
6480 Washington St. (Oak Circle), Yountville, 707-944-2070
◪ In Sonoma and Yountville, these "formulaic Italians" serve "standard fare" that shows "sparks of creativity" – primarily in "the amazing dipping oil they put on the table with sourdough"; while it's "nothing to write home" about and service can be "inattentive", it's a nice alternative to "higher-priced" options.

PINOT BLANC 🅻🅂🅼 22 22 21 $47
641 Main St. (Grayson Ave.), St. Helena, 707-963-6191
◪ Brought to you by chef Joachim Splichal's Patina group of LA, this "high-class" St. Helena haven offers "beautiful" surroundings "both indoors and out", "absolutely terrific" Cal–New French fare, a "great wine list and knowledgeable staff" – causing fans to fawn it's the "best underused restaurant in the Valley"; but a posse of disappointed devotees pout it's "overpriced and overrated" – "Joachim, where are you?"

Pizza Azzurro ⬛🅼 ▽ 22 14 18 $19
1400 Second St. (Franklin St.), Napa, 707-255-5552
■ It's "about time an affordable" source of "awesome" pies slathered with seasonal, regional ingredients "made its way to Downtown" say Napa natives grateful to this new "little cafe from a chef that used to cook at Tra Vigne"; the "young servers know how to take care of you" and the "upscale pizza-parlor atmosphere" makes it "an honest place to hang" "for that family-night out or quick lunch."

RAVENOUS ⑤   24 | 18 | 19 | $40
420 Center St. (North St.), Healdsburg, 707-431-1302
RAVENETTE ⚫⑤≠
117 North St. (bet. Center St. & Healdsburg Ave.), Healdsburg, 707-431-1770
◪ Last year the owners of this "locals' haunt" in Healdsburg moved their main eatery Ravenous to a larger location, saving the original site for mid-day meals; but while "lunch in Ravenette is still the best", some are "disappointed in dinner at the new place": yes, the Californian cuisine can be "truly ambrosial" and the setting, an "old house that glows with candles" and a patio "with twinkle lights in the trees", is "all charm"; but long waits ("even with reservations") and "uneven service" suggest it needs time "to adjust."

Ravens, The ⑤Ⓜ   ▽ 19 | 19 | 17 | $38
Stanford Inn by the Sea, 44850 Comptche-Ukiah Rd. (Coast Hwy. 1), Mendocino, 707-937-5615
■ "If you are – or ever have been – a vegetarian", this Mendocino eatery "will knock your socks off"; but even if you aren't, the "unusual preparations" (e.g. sea palm strudel), paired with a "nice view" of the organic gardens and the "enchanting sea", guarantees a good time.

Red Rock Cafe &   ▽ 23 | 9 | 16 | $17
Backdoor BBQ ⚫⑤Ⓜ
1010 Lincoln Ave. (Main St.), Napa, 707-226-2633
■ "Big messy burgers", "fantastic BBQ" and "family-size portions of" "fried stuff (fish 'n' chips, onion rings, etc.)" all rock at this "blue-collar" tavern in Downtown Napa; it gets "crowded at prime time, so watch for an open" "gingham-cloth" topped "table and run for it" or better still, head to the back door carry-out window "and take it home."

RENDEZVOUS INN &   24 | 19 | 23 | $41
RESTAURANT ⑤
647 N. Main St. (Bush St.), Fort Bragg, 707-964-8142
■ "Of all the places that dot the Mendocino coast, there are few that" "can beat chef-owner Kim Badenhop's passion

for food"; "rich in game", his "creative, delicious" New French fare paired with the "exemplary" yet "modestly priced wine list" makes this "high-class" Fort Bragg hostelry "one of the best deals" in the area.

RESTAURANT AT MEADOWOOD, THE 🅂🅜
23 | 25 | 23 | $55

Meadowood Resort, 900 Meadowood Ln. (Howell Mountain Rd., off Silverado Trail), St. Helena, 707-963-3646

■ "This place is heaven on earth and where the angels [must] eat" purr the pampered staying at St. Helena's "most luxurious inn"; set "amongst beautiful scenery" ("overlooking the golf course and croquet field"), the "service is exceptional", the Californian "tasting menu is generous" and the Napa Valley–oriented list "fabulous"; it's also "very expensive", but isn't all that "worth it?"

RESTAURANT AT STEVENSWOOD, THE 🅂🅜
26 | 24 | 24 | $54

Stevenswood Lodge, 8211 Shoreline Hwy./Hwy. 1 (2 mi. south of Mendocino), Little River, 707-937-2810

■ "Chef Marc Dym has raised the culinary bar on the North Coast" with his "stellar Continental gastronomy" that "is as good as SF's finest" (and "you will pay as much" for it); the combination of the "cozy", "art gallery-esque dining room [overlooking the] sculpture gardens" coupled with "perfectly orchestrated service" and arguably "the area's best wine list" "makes you hate to leave"; "fortunately it's customary to linger for hours fireside."

Restaurant 301 🅂🅜
▽ 25 | 22 | 25 | $43

The Carter House, 301 L St. (3rd St.), Eureka, 707-444-8062

■ "If you're passing through Eureka" you'll be "wonderfully surprised" to find "fine dining" in a "pleasant" Victorian inn; while it features "unusual and well-prepared" New French–New American fare (specializing in ingredients grown on the grounds) and "attentive service", it's the 3,500-bottle-rich wine list ("arguably the greatest cellar in the U.S.") "that's the star in this place."

Roux ▽ 26 | 19 | 24 | $45

1234 Main St. (Hunt Ave.), St. Helena, 707-963-5330
■ A "stunningly simple interior with white plates suspended on the [red] wall marks the scene of a stunningly wonderful restaurant" decree the culinary cognoscenti who come to this St. Helena sophomore; order the "four-course tasting menu" (with pairings from local boutique vintners) and your cup will runneth over with a series of "awesome" French-inspired American dishes (punctuated with "a series of *amuse-bouches* throughout") "served flawlessly by a fun group of people."

RUTHERFORD GRILL L S M 22 | 18 | 19 | $31

1180 Rutherford Rd. (Hwy. 29), Rutherford, 707-963-1792
☑ "If you've been indulging too much at the wineries, this "casual" Rutherford reliable is "a good place to overload on" all-American "iron-skillet cornbread" and "terrific ribs"; the no-reservations policy "really stinks" but the "no-corkage fee" is sweeter than the "Oreo cookie dessert", and while there are "better places in Napa Valley", none can compete with the dog-friendly patio (awarded "four paws" by our canine critics).

Sake Tini L S M ▽ 14 | 8 | 13 | $24

Bel Aire Plaza, 3900 Bel Aire Plaza (Trancas St.), Napa, 707-255-7423
☑ This hip sake specialist was "promising in its beginning" in 2000; but while many still think it's "fun to find" "interesting Asian food" "in an old bowling alley", others huff "there's not much atmosphere, sitting in a strip mall", saying it seems solely "to exist so that Napa twentysomethings can have a pick-up bar."

Santé S M – | – | – | E

(fka Restaurant at Sonoma Mission Inn & Spa)
Sonoma Mission Inn & Spa, 18140 Sonoma Hwy./Hwy. 12 (Boyes Blvd.), Sonoma, 707-939-2415
While few seem to recognize the Sonoma Mission Inn's recently rechristened eatery (amazing what these spa

getaways can do), those who have say the "new chef succeeds" with a *santé*-oriented cuisine that jettisons butter and cream for olive oil and wine; but you can still indulge in more standard Cal fare, much of it coaxed out of clay ovens.

SANTI L S M   23 | 18 | 21 | $39

21047 Geyserville Ave. (Hwy. 101), Geyserville, 707-857-1790
■ Northern Sonoma County visitors are "impressed" by this "SF caliber" "sleeper" that showcases a "hearty but elegant Italian cuisine" with a "strong" Cal-Ital "wine list to match" (most of the 'Cal' part is made up of local valley wines); "perfectly friendly and attentive" servers move through an area that boasts a "welcoming fireplace in cooler months, and a relaxing patio for the summer"; in short, "Geyserville may be the next Yountville if this keeps up."

Sassafras   ▽ 23 | 20 | 21 | $36
Restaurant & Wine Bar L S M
Santa Rosa Business Park, 1229 N. Dutton Ave. (College Ave.), Santa Rosa, 707-578-7600
■ Veteran restaurateur Michael Hirschberg has "nicely reincarnated" his Santa Rosa haunt, Mistral, with a little help from his friends: old chef Scott Synder, now turning out regional New American specialties (including a venison-pork terrine masquerading as a meatloaf sandwich), and returning wine director Laura Kudla, who oversees the exclusively born-in-the-USA list; already patrons praise the patio as a "great place to people-watch."

Sea Ranch Lodge   ▽ 16 | 21 | 19 | $37
Restaurant L S M
Sea Ranch Lodge, 60 Sea Walk Dr. (Hwy. 1), The Sea Ranch, 707-785-2371
■ Visitors who venture to this "remote" Sea Ranch resort are swept up by the "fabulous views and sunsets" "from any table in the house"; while the "landmark Northern California architecture" has long been the draw here, the kitchen offers "well-executed" Cal cuisine "with emphasis on [coastal] ingredients", aided by "friendly service."

Sharon's by the Sea 🇱🇸🇲 ▽ 21 | 16 | 20 | $28

32096 N. Harbor Dr. (Hwy. 1), Fort Bragg, 707-962-0680
■ When Mendocino coasters get "tired of high-class" dining, they "dress down" and go for Northern Italian-inflected fare, featuring "fresh fish off the boats", at this "seaside cafe" that "sits on the dock" of Noyo Harbor, aka "one of the cutest little working harbors you'll ever see."

ST. ORRES 🇸🇲 24 | 23 | 21 | $50

36601 Shoreline Hwy./Hwy. 1 (2 mi. north of Gualala), Gualala, 707-884-3303
◪ "Inspired by a woodland sprite", chef-owner Rosemary Campiformio "passionately forages" for chanterelles and other local goodies on the "unique" Cal menu served in her offbeat hostelry – "where else can you get a salad laced with red hots and jicama stars" while sitting amid a "Russian-style" residence complete with "onion domes and funky cottages"; the jaded find the show "tiring" ("relies more on quirky than quality"), but scores side with those who deem this "a wonderful place to eat and stay."

SYRAH 🇱 25 | 20 | 21 | $38

205 Fifth St. (Davis St.), Santa Rosa, 707-568-4002
■ Don't rely on syrah-ndipity to get yourself to this bistro, quickly becoming a Santa Rosa "hot spot" thanks to chef Josh Silver's "entertaining" personality and "imaginative" Californian-French fixings, "incredibly presented" in a "whimsical" dining room (upside down colanders serve as lighting fixtures); "the menu changes on a [monthly] basis", but you can count on "friendly service" (overseen by his wife/co-owner Regina) and *beaucoup* half-bottles of syrah (Rhône Valley varietals).

TASTINGS RESTAURANT 🇱🇸🇲 26 | 20 | 23 | $50

505 Healdsburg Ave. (Piper St.), Healdsburg, 707-433-3936
■ "Up-and-coming chef" Derek McCarthy and wife Sandy Kim's New American Healdsburg hideaway continues to wow "the wine-country set" by "turning out a sophisticated"

series of "small tastes" "inventively paired" – as the name implies – with "their unusual vino list"; diners dig the daily tasting menu that "allows you to sample many new things", while "the wonderful staff brings real class" and "warmth" "to a tough location" ("in a parking lot!").

TAYLOR'S AUTOMATIC REFRESHER L S M　　24 | 11 | 16 | $14 |

933 Main St. (bet. Charter Oak Ave. & Pope St.), St. Helena, 707-963-3486

■ "If you're driving through St. Helena", don't automatically pass by this "'50s-style" "drive-up diner", a refreshingly "unpretentious" "hamburger stand" with "thick milkshakes" that also "sells wine and takes American Express" (geez, "this is what makes people make fun of California"); the plastic comes in handy, 'cuz it may "look like fast food [but] it costs like white linen."

TERRA S M　　27 | 24 | 25 | $56 |

1345 Railroad Ave. (bet. Adams & Hunt Sts.), St. Helena, 707-963-8931

■ "Your taste buds have not yet been out of the closet until you've tried some of" chef/co-owner Hiro Sone's "absolutely unbelievable" "imaginative" New French fusion fare with Northern Italian and "Asian influences"; "the quiet old stone building" "off the main drag of St. Helena" offers "refuge from the wine country's marauding masses" with "gracious service" and an "out-of-this-world" vino list; so "let everyone duke it out to get reservations" elsewhere – this is a "true must-do" in the Valley.

Tomatina L S M　　15 | 10 | 11 | $19 |

Inn at Southbridge, 1016 Main St. (bet. Charter Oak Ave. & Pope St.), St. Helena, 707-967-9999

■ The fun, free-wheeling atmosphere of its namesake tomato food fight captures the spirit behind this "self-serve" Italian-Med; the "rockin'" *piadines* ("yummy flatbreads with a huge salad on top") and "chewy" wood-fired pizzas are the best bets for "budget meals" *con famiglia.*

TRA VIGNE L S M   25 | 25 | 21 | $46

1050 Charter Oak Ave. (Hwy. 29), St. Helena, 707-963-4444
☑ Chef "Michael Chiarello is gone" but "this Napa Valley tradition" still "shines" with "absolutely glorious", "daring combinations" of Californian-Italian food; despite somewhat "haughty" hosts, the "knowledgeable, friendly staff helps you choose" from the "impeccable" wine list; the dining room "is reminiscent of an Italian cathedral" but "you may need to genuflect to" snare "a table in the summer" on the "idyllic outdoor patio among the vines" (if you can't, "try eating at the bar and catch up on all the vineyard dirt").

Tuscany L S M   16 | 20 | 15 | $37

1005 First St. (Main St.), Napa, 707-258-1000
☑ Now into its second season, this Napa trattoria continues to fill up with "wine country locals" who find it "fun to sit at the counter and watch" the "masters of the wood-fired oven" at work; however, while the "beautiful large room" "smells good", "nothing sparkles" on the Northern Italian menu, and "they still don't take reservations."

Uva Trattoria Italiana L S   – | – | – | M

1040 Clinton St. (Main St.), Napa, 707-255-6646
The name remains the same, but a dynamic duo of Italian-blooded Napa natives intends to transform this affordable trattoria into a more lively Downtown destination; new chef Jude Wilmouth (ex Tra Vigne) has introduced classic Southern Italian items like pan-roasted Chianti-marinated rabbit; an enlarged bar serves a new small-plates menu, too.

Victorian Gardens S   ▽ 29 | 28 | 30 | $65

Victorian Gardens, 14409 S. Hwy. 1 (south of Elk, 8 mi. north of Pt. Arena), Manchester, 707-882-3606
■ "An evening spent" at this "exquisitely restored Victorian" inn on the Mendocino coast is an "opulent affair" to "be remembered for years"; chef/co-owner Luciano Zamboni prepares a five-course tasting menu featuring Italian wines and "food from a Roman nonna's kitchen" (and "harvested from his incredible garden" and livestock farm), while his

wife Pauline "gives you the most personal service you ever encountered"; plus there's only one seating a night, so you can linger as long as Victoria's reign.

Villa Corona **L S**   ▽ 20 | 9 | 16 | $14

Bel Aire Plaza, 3614 Bel Aire Plaza (Trancas St.), Napa, 707-257-8685
1138 Main St. (bet. Pope & Spring Sts.), St. Helena, 707-963-7812 **M**

■ "If you're hungry for authentic Mexican food" when traveling in wine country, these "family-run" cantinas in Napa and St. Helena provide a *Like Water for Chocolate* experience with "awesome guacamole", "carnitas burritos that are almost all meat" and "addictive enchiladas"; "speedy counter ordering" is the crowning touch.

Wappo Bar Bistro **L S M**   21 | 21 | 19 | $33

1226 Washington St. (Lincoln Ave.), Calistoga, 707-942-4712

◪ An "interesting blend of cuisines" equals a "delightful" meal at this International "find in Calistoga" complemented by a "good wine list with a few lesser-known labels" but without the whopping mark-ups; "sitting outside under the grape arbor for lunch" (and on summer nights) "is divine" and is a superior alternative to the "crowded" digs inside, but be warned: "service can be a bit flaky."

Water Street Bistro **L S M** ⬚   – | – | – | M

100 Petaluma Blvd. N. (Western Ave.), Petaluma, 707-763-9563
This French bistro facing the Petaluma River and run by Stephanie Rastetter (the "excellent chef" from the now-shuttered Babette's) offers "fabulous", "fresh" sandwiches, soups and salads in a "pleasant", "casual" setting; N.B. although the kitchen closes at 5 PM, it serves summertime suppers on Friday and Saturday and monthly theme dinners.

Willow Wood Market Cafe **L S M**   21 | 13 | 16 | $22

9020 Graton Rd. (bet. Brush & Edison Sts.), Graton, 707-522-8372
■ "Tucked" away "in a funky little grocery store" "in the one-horse town of Graton", this "eclectic" eatery whipping

up "country comfort food" and International eats ("great polenta") is the "locals' favorite" for "non-traditional breakfasts" and "creative sandwiches"; you've got to be "willing to wait", because it doesn't take reservations and the service can be as "relaxed" as the "atmosphere."

WINE SPECTATOR GREYSTONE 🅛🅢🅜   22 | 23 | 20 | $47

Culinary Institute of America, 2555 Main St. (Deer Park Rd.), St. Helena, 707-967-1010

◪ This "stately château" in St. Helena is "as much of a tourist attraction as the wineries" which surround it; the "cavernous" interior features "wonderful" chef-watching in the open kitchen where "delightful seasonal" Cal fare is prepared; given that it's "run by CIA" (the cooking school, "not the spies"), it's not surprising that the staff is "knowledgeable"; however, bi-coastal bashers deem it "disappointing compared to its Hyde Park, NY, counterpart."

zazu 🅢   ▽ 26 | 19 | 24 | $43

(fka zuzu)
3535 Guerneville Rd. (Willowside Rd.), Santa Rosa, 707-523-4814

■ Although this Santa Rosa sophomore was forced to change its name last year, that hasn't stopped its "talented" husband-and-wife team from creating perhaps the "most memorable", "exciting" "unfussy, yet sophisticated" Italian– New American cuisine with an "extensive local wine selection"; the "cozy, easy-going atmosphere" makes you feel comfortable enough to "go in jeans or Chanel."

Zin 🅛🅢🅜   20 | 17 | 20 | $37

344 Center St. (North St.), Healdsburg, 707-473-0946

◪ "Zin is in" at this viticultural venue located just off Healdsburg Square showcasing "an extensive Sonoma Zinfandel list" and "hearty", "zinful" New American food to pair with it; while the fare is "not for light eaters" (think ribs and beer-battered green beans), "it's honest" and "fun", much like the "friendly staff"; however, the "industrial decor" gives the zin-sation of an "empty warehouse."

Zinsvalley 🅛🅜   – | – | – | M

Browns Valley Mkt., 3253 Browns Valley Rd. (bet. Austin & Larkin Sts.), Napa, 707-224-0695

This off-the-beaten-track sophomore may not be the best-known "in Browns Valley", but it has "quickly become one of the area's favorites" thanks to the deft touch of its Mustards-alumni management; the converted home offers Eclectic-American eats served in two cozy rooms with loads of brick, wood and fireplaces or on a large patio overlooking a creek; true to its name, the wine list features 60 Zinfandels (many of which are small producers).

ZUZU 🅛🅢🅜   22 | 20 | 22 | $34

829 Main St. (bet. 2nd & 3rd Sts.), Napa, 707-224-8555

■ Arriving just in time for the revitalization of old-town Napa, this "happening" "hot spot" is "a nibbler's dream" offering an array of affordable traditional Spanish tapas along with "innovative" "small dishes" from South and Central America; a wormwood bar, sultry Corona-red plaster walls and "dimly lit" Moroccan lamps lend a lived-in feel to the bi-level "hangout"; N.B. don't confuse this with Santa Rosa's zazu, which bore the same name for a short time.

CUISINES

American (New)

Alexis Baking Co.
Bistro at Glen Ellen
Bistro Ralph
Boonville Hotel
Brannan's Grill
Cafe La Haye
Cafe Lolo
Celadon
Deuce
Dry Creek Kitchen
Duck Club
Feast
French Laundry
Kenwood
Martini House
Mendo Bistro
Miramonte
Mirepoix
Mustards Grill
955 Ukiah
Restaurant 301
Roux
Sassafras
Tastings Rest.
zazu
Zin
Zinsvalley

American (Traditional)

Calistoga Inn
Felix & Louie's
FlatIron Grill
Gordon's
Jimtown Store
Lauren's
Rutherford Grill
Taylor's Automatic

Asian

Lisa Hemenway's Bistro
Pairs
Sake Tini

Bakeries

Alexis Baking Co.
Costeaux Bakery
Downtown Bakery
Model Bakery

Barbecue

Foothill Cafe
Geyersville Smokehouse
Red Rock Cafe

Californian

Albion River Inn
All Season's Cafe
Applewood Inn
Boonville Hotel

Cuisine Index

Brix
Cafe Beaujolais
Cafe Lucy
Carneros
Charcuterie
Chateau Souverain
Domaine Chandon
Farmhouse Inn
Foothill Cafe
General's Daughter
Glen Ellen Inn
John Ash & Co.
Julia's Kitchen
Ledford House
Little River Inn
Lucy's Rest.
MacCallum House
Madrona Manor
Meadowood Grill
Mixx Rest.
Moosse Cafe
Napa Valley Grille
Napa Valley Wine Train
Osake
Pairs
Pearl
Pinot Blanc
Ravenette
Ravenous
Rest. at Meadowood
Santé

Sea Ranch Lodge
St. Orres
Syrah
Tra Vigne
Wine Spectator Greystone

Chinese
Gary Chu

Coffee Shops/Diners
Downtown Bakery

Continental
Rest. at Stevenswood

Delis/Sandwich Shops
Downtown Bakery
Jimtown Store

Eclectic/International
Bistro at Glen Ellen
Cafe La Haye
Cafe Prima
Lauren's
Pangaea
Wappo Bar Bistro
Willow Wood Market
Zinsvalley

French
Auberge du Soleil
Cafe Beaujolais
Chateau Souverain

Costeaux Bakery
French Laundry

French (Bistro)

Bistro Jeanty
Bouchon
Cafe Lucy
Charcuterie
girl & the fig
K&L Bistro
Syrah
Water Street Bistro

French (New)

All Season's Cafe
Applewood Inn
Domaine Chandon
Julia's Kitchen
Kenwood
La Toque
Lisa Hemenway's Bistro
Madrona Manor
Marché aux Fleurs
Mirepoix
955 Ukiah
Pinot Blanc
Rendezvous Inn
Restaurant 301
Roux
Terra

Fusion

Brix
Terra

Hamburgers

Red Rock Cafe
Taylor's Automatic

Italian

(N=Northern; S=Southern;
N&S=includes both)
Bistro Don Giovanni (N&S)
Cafe Citti (N)
Cucina Paradiso (S)
Cucina Viansa (N)
Della Santina's (N)
Felix & Louie's (N&S)
Graziano's Rist. (N&S)
Green Valley Cafe (N)
Piatti (N&S)
Santi (N&S)
Sharon's by the Sea (N)
Tomatina (N&S)
Tra Vigne (N&S)
Tuscany (N)
Uva Trattoria (N&S)
Victorian Gardens (N&S)
zazu (N)

Japanese

Hana Japanese
Osake

Cuisine Index

Mediterranean
Auberge du Soleil
Carneros
Celadon
Ledford House
Lucy's Rest.
Manzanita
Mendo Bistro
Tomatina

Mexican/Tex-Mex
Maya
Villa Corona

Pizza
Pizza Azzurro

Portuguese
LaSalette

Pub Food
Calistoga Inn

Seafood
Sharon's by the Sea

South American
girl & the gaucho
Miramonte

Southern/Soul
Catahoula Rest.

Spanish
Zuzu

Steakhouses
Cole's Chop House

Tapas
girl & the gaucho
Zuzu

Vegetarian
Ravens

Vietnamese
Pho Vietnam

LOCATIONS

Calistoga
All Season's Cafe
Brannan's Grill
Calistoga Inn
Catahoula Rest.
FlatIron Grill
Wappo Bar Bistro

Eureka
Restaurant 301

Geyserville
Geyserville Smokehouse
Santi

Glen Ellen/Kenwood
Bistro at Glen Ellen
Cafe Citti
girl & the gaucho
Glen Ellen Inn
Kenwood

Guerneville
Applewood Inn
Farmhouse Inn

Healdsburg
Bistro Ralph
Charcuterie
Costeaux Bakery
Downtown Bakery
Dry Creek Kitchen

Felix & Louie's
Jimtown Store
Madrona Manor
Manzanita
Ravenette
Ravenous
Tastings Rest.
Zin

Mendocino County
Albion River Inn
Boonville Hotel
Cafe Beaujolais
Cafe Prima
Lauren's
Ledford House
Little River Inn
MacCallum House
Mendo Bistro
Moosse Cafe
955 Ukiah
Pangaea
Ravens
Rendezvous Inn
Rest. at Stevenswood
Sea Ranch Lodge
Sharon's by the Sea
St. Orres
Victorian Gardens

Location Index

LaSalette
Maya
Piatti
Santé

Sonoma Coast
Duck Club

St. Helena
Green Valley Cafe
Martini House
Meadowood Grill
Miramonte
Model Bakery
Pinot Blanc
Rest. at Meadowood
Roux

Taylor's Automatic
Terra
Tomatina
Tra Vigne
Villa Corona
Wine Spectator Greystone

Yountville
Bistro Jeanty
Bouchon
Domaine Chandon
French Laundry
Gordon's
Napa Valley Grille
Piatti

Napa Wineries

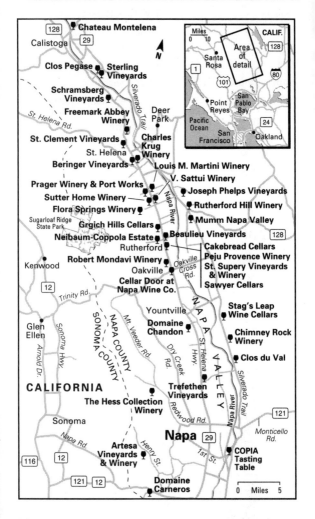

Chateau Montelena

Calistoga

Clos Pegase • Sterling Vineyards

Schramsberg Vineyards

Freemark Abbey Winery

Deer Park

St. Helena Rd.

St. Clement Vineyards

St. Helena

Charles Krug Winery

Beringer Vineyards

Louis M. Martini Winery

V. Sattui Winery

Prager Winery & Port Works

Joseph Phelps Vineyards

Sutter Home Winery

Rutherford Hill Winery

Flora Springs Winery

Mumm Napa Valley

Sugarloaf Ridge State Park

Grgich Hills Cellars

Beaulieu Vineyards

Neibaum-Coppola Estate

Rutherford

Cakebread Cellars

Kenwood

Robert Mondavi Winery

Oakville Cross Rd.

Peju Provence Winery

St. Supery Vineyards & Winery

Oakville

Sawyer Cellars

Cellar Door at Napa Wine Co.

Stag's Leap Wine Cellars

Yountville

Glen Ellen

Domaine Chandon

Chimney Rock Winery

Clos du Val

CALIFORNIA

The Hess Collection Winery

Trefethen Vineyards

Sonoma

Napa

COPIA Tasting Table

Artesa Vineyards & Winery

Domaine Carneros

Silverado Trail

Napa River

NAPA COUNTY

SONOMA COUNTY

Mt. Veeder Rd.

Dry Creek Rd.

St. Helena Hwy.

Redwood Rd.

Napa River

Silverado Trail

NAPA VALLEY

Monticello Rd.

Trinity Rd.

Sonoma Hwy.

Arnold Dr.

Napa Rd.

Henry St.

1st St.

128

29

12

128

121

116

12

121

12

Miles
0   10

CALIF.

Santa Rosa

Area of detail

128

80

Point Reyes

San Pablo Bay

24

Pacific Ocean

San Francisco

Oakland

1

101

0   Miles   5

Sonoma Wineries

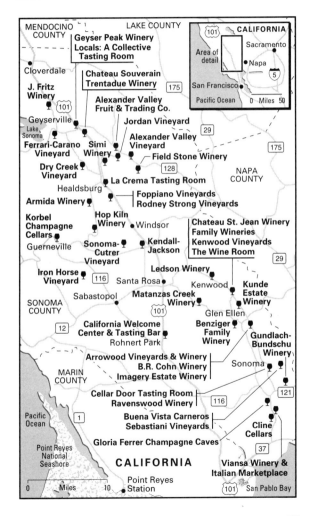

MENDOCINO COUNTY
LAKE COUNTY

CALIFORNIA
101
Area of detail
Sacramento
Napa
5
San Francisco
Pacific Ocean
0 Miles 50

Geyser Peak Winery
Locals: A Collective Tasting Room

Cloverdale

J. Fritz Winery

Chateau Souverain
Trentadue Winery
175

Alexander Valley Fruit & Trading Co.

Geyserville
101

Jordan Vineyard

Lake Sonoma

Ferrari-Carano Vineyard
Simi Winery
Alexander Valley Vineyard
29
Field Stone Winery
175

Dry Creek Vineyard
128
NAPA COUNTY

Healdsburg
La Crema Tasting Room

Armida Winery
Foppiano Vineyards
Rodney Strong Vineyards

Korbel Champagne Cellars
Hop Kiln Winery
Windsor
Chateau St. Jean Winery
Family Wineries
Kenwood Vineyards
The Wine Room

Guerneville
Sonoma-Cutrer Vineyard
Kendall-Jackson
29

Iron Horse Vineyard
116
Ledson Winery

Santa Rosa
Kenwood
Kunde Estate Winery

SONOMA COUNTY
Sabastopol
Matanzas Creek Winery
101
Glen Ellen

12
California Welcome Center & Tasting Bar
Rohnert Park
Benziger Family Winery
Gundlach-Bundschu Winery

Arrowood Vineyards & Winery
B.R. Cohn Winery
Imagery Estate Winery
Sonoma
121

MARIN COUNTY

Cellar Door Tasting Room
Ravenswood Winery
116

Pacific Ocean
Buena Vista Carneros
Sebastiani Vineyards
Cline Cellars

1
Gloria Ferrer Champagne Caves
37

Point Reyes National Seashore
CALIFORNIA
Viansa Winery & Italian Marketplace

0 Miles 10
Point Reyes Station
101
San Pablo Bay

Mendocino Wineries

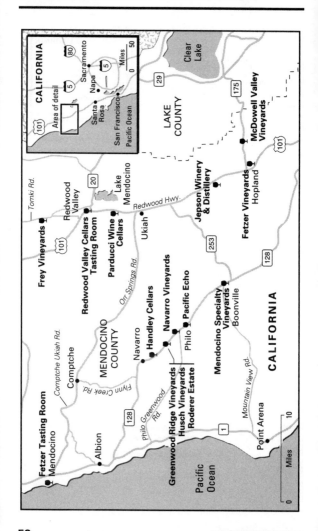

WINERIES & TASTING ROOMS

Napa County

Artesa Vineyards & Winery
1345 Henry Rd., Napa, 707-224-1668;
www.artesawinery.com

Beaulieu Vineyards
1960 St. Helena Hwy., Rutherford, 707-963-2411; 800-264-6918;
www.bvwine.com

Beringer Vineyards
2000 Main St., St. Helena, 707-963-7115;
www.beringer.com

Cakebread Cellars
8300 St. Helena Hwy., Rutherford, 707-963-5221;
800-588-0298; www.cakebread.com

Cellar Door at Napa Wine Co.
7830-40 St. Helena Hwy., Oakville, 707-944-1710; 800-848-9630;
www.napawineco.com

Charles Krug Winery
2800 Main St., St. Helena, 707-963-5057; 800-237-0033;
www.charleskrug.com

Chateau Montelena
1429 Tubbs Ln., Calistoga, 707-942-5105;
www.montelena.com

Chimney Rock Winery
5340 Silverado Trail, Napa, 707-257-2641; 800-257-2641;
www.chimneyrock.com

Clos du Val
5330 Silverado Trail, Napa, 707-259-2200; 800-993-9463;
www.closduval.com

Clos Pegase
1060 Dunaweal Ln., Calistoga, 707-942-4981; 800-366-8583;
www.clospegase.com

COPIA Tasting Table
500 First St., Napa, 707-265-1600; www.copia.org

Domaine Carneros
1240 Duhig Rd., Napa, 707-257-0101; www.domaine.com

Domaine Chandon
1 California Dr., Yountville, 707-944-2280; 800-934-3975;
www.chandon.com

Flora Springs Winery
1978 West Zinfandel Ln., St. Helena, 707-963-5711;
www.florasprings.com

Freemark Abbey Winery
3022 St. Helena Hwy. N., St. Helena, 707-963-9694; 800-963-9698;
www.freemarkabbey.com

Grgich Hills Cellars
1829 St. Helena Hwy., Rutherford, 707-963-2784; 800-532-3057;
www.grgich.com

Hess Collection Winery, The
4411 Redwood Rd., Napa, 707-255-1144;
www.hesscollection.com

Joseph Phelps Vineyards
200 Taplin Rd., St. Helena, 707-963-2745; 800-707-5789;
www.jpvwines.com

Louis M. Martini Winery
254 St. Helena Hwy., St. Helena, 707-963-2736; 800-321-9463;
www.louismartini.com

Mumm Napa Valley
8445 Silverado Trail, Rutherford, 707-942-3434;
www.mummcuveenapa.com

Niebaum-Coppola Estate
1991 St. Helena Hwy., Rutherford, 707-968 1100; 800-782-4266;
www.niebaum-coppola.com

Peju Province Winery
8466 St. Helena Hwy., Rutherford, 707-963-3600;
800-446-7358; www.peju.com

Prager Winery & Port Works
1281 Lewelling Ln., St. Helena, 707-963-7678; 800-969-7678;
www.pragerport.com

Robert Mondavi Winery
7801 St. Helena Hwy., Oakville, 707-963-9611; 888-766-6328;
www.robertmondavi.com

Rutherford Hill Winery
200 Rutherford Hill Rd., Rutherford, 707-963-1871; 800-637-5681;
www.rutherfordhill.com

Sawyer Cellars
8350 St. Helena Hwy., Rutherford, 707-963-1980;
www.sawyercellars.com

Schramsberg Vineyards
1400 Schramsberg Rd., Calistoga, 707-942-2414; 707-942-6668;
800-877-3623; www.schramsberg.com

Stag's Leap Wine Cellars
5766 Silverado Trail, Napa, 707-265-2441; 866-422-7523;
www.cask23.com

St. Clement Vineyards
2867 St. Helena Hwy. N., St. Helena, 707-963-4507; 800-331-8266;
www.stclement.com

Sterling Vineyards
1111 Dunaweal Ln., Calistoga, 707-942-3344;
www.sterlingvineyards.com

St. Supery Vineyards & Winery
8440 St. Helena Hwy., Rutherford, 707-963-4507; 800-942-0809;
www.stsupery.com

Sutter Home Winery
277 St. Helena Hwy. S., St. Helena, 707-963-3104 x4208;
www.sutterhome.com

Trefethen Vineyards
1160 Oak Knoll Ave., Napa, 707-255-7700

V. Sattui Winery
1111 White Ln., St. Helena, 707-963-7774; 800-799-2337;
www.vsattui.com

Sonoma County

Alexander Valley Fruit & Trading Co.
5110 Hwy. 128, Geyserville, 707-433-1944

Alexander Valley Vineyards
8644 Hwy. 128, Healdsburg, 707-433-7209; 800-888-7209;
www.avvwine.com

Armida Winery
2201 Westside Rd., Healdsburg, 707-433-2222;
www.armida.com

Arrowood Vineyards & Winery
14347 Sonoma Hwy., Glen Ellen, 707-938-5170; 800-938-5170;
www.arrowoodwinery.com

Benziger Family Winery
1883 London Ranch Rd., Glen Ellen, 707-935-3000;
www.benziger.com

B.R. Cohn Winery
15000 Sonoma Hwy., Glen Ellen, 707-938-4064; 800-330-4064;
www.brcohn.com

Buena Vista Carneros
18000 Old Winery Rd., Sonoma, 707-938-1266;
www.buenavistawinery.com

California Welcome Center and Tasting Bar
5000 Roberts Lake Rd., Rohnert Park, 707-586-3795;
800-939-7666; www.sonomawine.com

Cellar Door Tasting Room, The
The Lodge at Sonoma, 1395 Broadway Suite E., Sonoma,
707-938-4466

Chateau Souverain
400 Souverain Rd., Geyserville, 707-433-8281; 888-809-4637;
www.chateausouverain.com

Chateau St. Jean and Winery
8555 Sonoma Hwy. 12, Kenwood, 707-833-4134; 800-543-7572;
www.chateaustjean.com

Cline Cellars
24737 Arnold Dr./Hwy. 121, Sonoma, 707-935-4310; 800-546-2070;
www.clinecellars.com

Dry Creek Vineyard
3770 Lambert Bridge Rd., Healdsburg, 707-433-1000;
800-864-9463; www.drycreekvineyard.com

Family Wineries of Sonoma
9200 Sonoma Hwy. 12, Kenwood, 707-833-5504

Ferrari-Carano Vineyards & Winery
8761 Dry Creek Rd., Healdsburg, 707-433-6700;
www.ferrari-carano.com

Field Stone Winery & Vineyard
10075 Hwy. 128, Healdsburg, 707-433-7266; 800-544-7273;
www.fieldstonewinery.com

Foppiano Vineyards
12707 Old Redwood Hwy., Healdsburg, 707-433-7272;
www.foppiano.com

Geyser Peak Winery
22281 Chianti Rd., Geyserville, 707-857-9400; 800-255-9463;
www.geyserpeakwinery.com

Gloria Ferrer Champagne Caves
23555 Hwy. 121, Sonoma, 707-996-7256;
www.gloriaferrer.com

Gundlach-Bundschu Winery
2000 Denmark St., Sonoma, 707-938-5277; www.gunbun.com

Hop Kiln Winery
6050 Westside Rd., Healdsburg, 707-433-6491;
www.hopkilnwinery.com

Imagery Estate Winery
14335 Hwy. 12, Glen Ellen, 877-550-4278; 800-989-8890;
www.imagerywinery.com

Iron Horse Vineyards
9786 Ross Station Rd., Sebastopol, 707-887-1507;
www.ironhorsevineyards.com

J. Fritz Winery
24691 Dutcher Creek Rd., Cloverdale, 707-894-3389;
www.fritzwinery.com

Jordan Vineyard and Winery
1474 Alexander Valley Rd., Healdsburg, 707-431-5247;
800-654-1213; www.jordanwinery.com

Kendall-Jackson Wine Center
5007 Fulton Rd., Santa Rosa, 707-571-7500; www.kj.com

Kenwood Vineyards
9592 Sonoma Hwy. 12, Kenwood, 707-833-5891;
www.kenwoodvineyards.com

Korbel Champagne Cellars
13250 River Rd., Guerneville, 707-887-2294; 800-656-7235;
www.korbel.com

Kunde Estate Winery
10155 Sonoma Hwy. 12, Kenwood, 707-833-5501;
www.kunde.com

La Crema Tasting Room
337 Healdsburg Ave., Healdsburg, 707-433-4474

Ledson Winery
7335 Hwy. 12, Santa Rosa, 707-537-3810; www.ledson.com

Locals: A Collective Tasting Room
21023A Geyserville Ave., Geyserville, 707-857-4900;
www.tastelocalwine.com

Matanzas Creek Winery
6097 Bennett Valley Rd., Santa Rosa, 707-823-2404;
800-590-6464; www.matanzascreek.com

Ravenswood Winery
18701 Gehricke Rd., Sonoma, 707-938-1960;
www.ravenswood-wine.com

Rodney Strong Vineyards
11455 Old Redwood Hwy., Healdsburg, 707-431-1533;
800-678-4763; www.rodneystrong.com

Sebastiani Vineyards
389 Fourth St. E., Sonoma, 707-933-3200; www.sebastiani.com

Simi Winery
16275 Healdsburg Ave., Healdsburg, 707-433-6981;
www.simiwinery.com

Sonoma-Cutrer Vineyards
4401 Slusser Rd., Windsor, 707-528-1181;
www.sonomacutrer.com

Trentadue Winery & Vineyards
19170 Geyserville Ave., Geyserville, 707-433-3104; 888-332-3032;
www.trentadue.com

Viansa Winery & Italian Marketplace
25200 Hwy. 121, Sonoma, 707-935-4700; www.viansa.com

Wine Room, The
9575 Sonoma Hwy., Kenwood, 707-833-4455;
www.the-wine-room.com

Mendocino County

Fetzer Tasting Room
45070 Main St., Mendocino, 707-937-6190; www.fetzer.com

Fetzer Vineyards
13601 Eastside Rd., Hopland, 707-744-1250; www.fetzer.com

Frey Vineyards
14000 Tomki Rd., Redwood Valley, 707-485-5177; 800-760-3739;
www.freywine.com

Greenwood Ridge Vineyards
5501 Hwy. 128, Philo, 707-895-2002

Handley Cellars
3151 Hwy. 128, Philo, 707-895-3876; 800-733-3151;
www.handleycellars.com

Husch Vineyards
4400 Hwy. 128, Philo, 707-895-3216; 800-554-8724;
www.huschvineyards.com

Jepson, Winery and Distillery
10400 S. Hwy. 101, Ukiah, 707-468-8936; 800-516-7342;
www.jepsonwine.com

McDowell Valley Vineyards
3811 Hwy. 175, Hopland, 707-744-1053;
www.mcdowellsyrah.com

Mendocino Specialty Vineyards
17810 Farrer Ln., Boonville, 707-895-3993; 800-537-9463

Navarro Vineyards
5601 Hwy. 128, Philo, 707-895-3686; www.navarrowine.com

Pacific Echo
8501 Hwy. 128, Philo, 707-895-2957; www.pacific-echo.com

Parducci Wine Cellars
501 Parducci Rd., Ukiah; 888-362-9463; www.parducci.com

Redwood Valley Cellars Tasting Room
7051 N. State St., Redwood Valley, 707-485-0322

Roderer Estate
4501 Hwy. 128, Philo, 707-895-2288; www.roederer-estate.com

For more information:

Napa Valley Vintners Association
707-963-3388; www.napavintners.com

Sonoma Valley Vintners & Growers Alliance
17964 Sonoma Hwy., Sonoma, 707-935-0803;
www.sonomavalleywine.com

Mendocino Winegrowers Alliance
P.O. Box 1409, Ukiah, 707-468-9886; www.mendowine.com

Wine Vintage Chart

Prepared by our friend Howard Stravitz, this chart is designed to help you select wine to go with your meal.

	'85	'86	'88	'89	'90	'94	'95	'96	'97	'98	'99	'00	'01
WHITES													
French:													
Alsace	24	18	22	28	28	26	25	23	23	25	23	25	26
Burgundy	26	25	17	25	24	15	29	28	25	24	25	22	20
Loire Valley	–	–	–	–	25	23	24	26	24	23	24	25	23
Champagne	28	25	24	26	29	–	26	27	24	24	25	25	–
Sauternes	21	28	29	25	27	–	20	23	27	22	22	22	28
California (Napa, Sonoma, Mendocino):													
Chardonnay	–	–	–	–	–	22	27	23	27	25	25	23	26
Sauvignon Blanc/Semillon	–	–	–	–	–	–	–	–	24	24	25	22	26
REDS													
French:													
Bordeaux	25	26	24	27	29	22	26	25	23	24	23	25	23
Burgundy	23	–	21	25	28	–	26	27	25	22	27	22	20
Rhône	25	19	27	29	29	24	25	23	25	28	26	27	24
Beaujolais	–	–	–	–	–	–	–	–	23	22	25	25	18
California (Napa, Sonoma, Mendocino):													
Cab./Merlot	26	26	–	21	28	29	27	25	28	23	26	23	26
Pinot Noir	–	–	–	–	–	27	24	24	26	25	26	25	27
Zinfandel	–	–	–	–	–	25	22	23	21	22	24	19	24
Italian:													
Tuscany	26	–	24	–	26	22	25	20	28	24	27	26	25
Piedmont	26	–	26	28	29	–	23	26	28	26	25	24	22

And for your
next course...

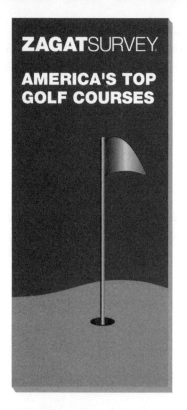

Introducing America's Top Golf Courses, rated and reviewed by avid golfers. Besides telling you what the courses and facilities are like, we'll tell you how much you'll pay and even how well you'll eat.

Available wherever books are sold, at zagat.com
or by calling **888-371-5440.**